THE STATUE OF LIBERTY

Author: Holly Karapetkova

Rourke Publishing LLC
Vero Beach, Florida 32964

© 2009 Rourke Publishing LLC

All rights reserved. No part of this book may be reproduced or used in any form or by any means, electronic or mechanical, including photocopying, recording, or by any information storage and retrieval system without permission in writing from the publisher.

www.rourkepublishing.com

PHOTO CREDITS: © James Kingman: page 4; © Library Of Congress: page 5, 7, 10, 13, 14,15, 16, 17, 20, 21, 22, 24, 25, 26; © Ufuk ZIVANA: page 7; © Nicolas Sanchez: page 9; © National Park Service: page 8, 9, 28; © HultonArchive: page 11 © Zbigniew Majerczyk: page 12; © Michael Cavén: page 13; Wikipedia.com: page 11, 15, 22; © Thomas Nord: page 16; © Bryan Busovicki; © Jaap2: page 23; @ Library of Congress Bill Manning: page 25; © LOU OATES: oval frame page 27; © ExaMedia Photography: page 29; © Denise Lafferty: page 29; © Donald R. Swartz: page 29, 30.

Editor: Jeanne Sturm

Cover Design: Nicola Stratford: bdpublishing.com

Page Design: Renee Brady

Library of Congress Cataloging-in-Publication Data

Karapetkova, Holly.
 The Statue of Liberty / Holly Karapetkova.
     p. cm. -- (American symbols and landmarks)
 ISBN 978-1-60472-345-8 (Hardcover)
 ISBN 978-1-60472-975-7 (Softcover)
 1. Statue of Liberty (New York, N.Y.)--Juvenile literature.
 F128.64.L6 K37 2009
 974.7/1 22
                                            2008014138

Printed in the USA

IG/IG

Rourke Publishing

www.rourkepublishing.com – rourke@rourkepublishing.com
Post Office Box 3328, Vero Beach, FL 32964

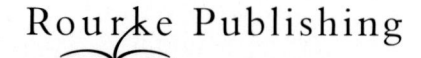

Table of Contents

A Symbol of Freedom and Opportunity 4

The Origins of Liberty 6

Financing Liberty 10

Building Liberty 14

Gigantic Proportions 18

The Statue's Symbols 19

Liberty Arrives in America 20

Ellis Island 24

A Poem for Liberty 26

Changes and Renovations 28

Visiting the Statue of Liberty National Monument . . 30

Glossary 31

Index 32

A Symbol of Freedom and Opportunity

The Statue of Liberty Enlightening the World was given to the United States as a gift from France over one hundred years ago.

Today, the statue continues to celebrate the freedom and independence that America represents to people around the world. She stands on a small island in New York Harbor near Ellis Island, where immigrants once entered the country seeking freedom from social, political, and economic troubles.

When the immigrants arrived in our country, they were greeted by the Statue, who promised them liberty and a new life. Thus, the Statue has come to represent the open arms that America holds out to people who come here seeking freedom and opportunity.

5

The Origins of Liberty

It was the summer of 1875, almost 100 years since the founding fathers had signed the Declaration of Independence and given birth to the United States of America. A man named Edouard de Laboulaye, a lawyer and teacher who admired America's strength and ideals, held a party at his home in France.

At his party, Laboulaye discussed building a monument that would celebrate America's 100 years of independence. France had helped America achieve its independence from the British in the Revolutionary War. Laboulaye felt a statue that combined the efforts of both the Americans and the French would be a perfect symbol of the friendship between the two countries.

Edouard de Laboulaye

France's flag is sometimes called the Tricolor. It was first created in 1790 during the French Revolution.

A young sculptor at his party, Frederic Auguste Bartholdi, heard his idea and was excited about a monument to liberty. He spoke with Laboulaye and decided to travel to America to see if people there would also be excited about the idea. While he was there, he sailed into New York Harbor and saw Bedloe's Island (today known as Liberty Island) and his imagination caught fire.

He would build a gigantic statue that would be seen by everyone traveling to America and entering the harbor. It would be a statue of a woman named Liberty, towering over the city of New York as a reminder of the principles upon which the nation was founded.

The Mind Behind the Statue

Frederic Auguste Bartholdi was born in France in 1834. He studied art from a very early age and designed his first monument when he was only 19 years old. He traveled to Egypt and was inspired by the great size and scale of the Sphinx and the pyramids. Bartholdi liked his art to be "broad, massive, and simple," as he once told a reporter, and the gigantic Statue of Liberty turned out to be the perfect project for him. He also created many other monuments and sculptures in France throughout his life.

Le Lion de Belfort (The Lion of Belfort) 1872-1879

Frederic Auguste Bartholdi

Financing Liberty

Since the Statue of Liberty would represent the friendship between America and France, it was important for both countries to contribute to the costs and effort of building the statue. France would finance and build the statue itself, while America would finance and build the base for the statue.

In France, people held lotteries and put on events like banquets and operas to fundraise for the statue. They managed to raise enough to build the monument.

Bartholdi's design patent, shown here, was issued in 1879.

Horse-drawn buses carry passengers outside the opera house in Paris, France.

New York

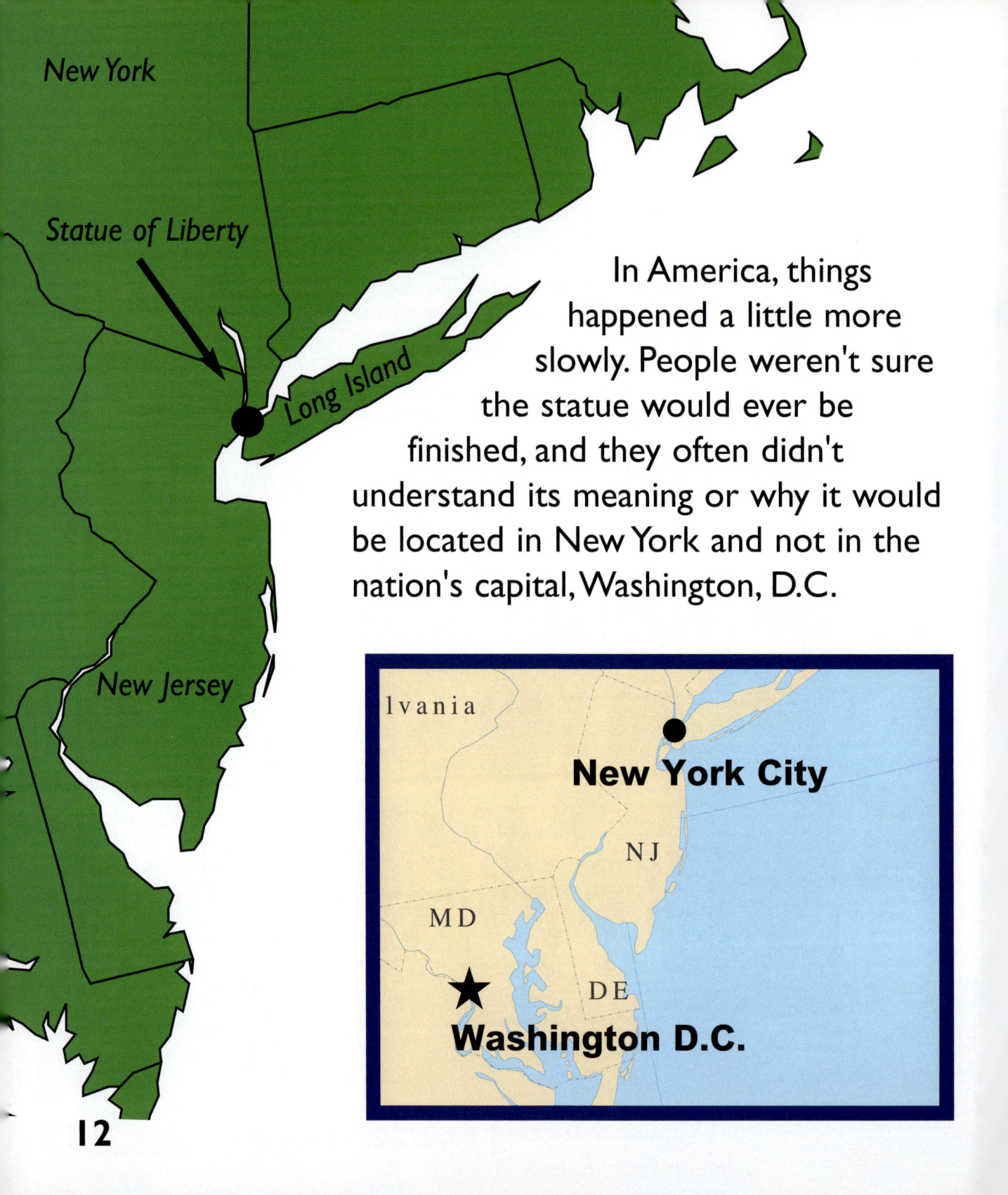

Statue of Liberty

Long Island

New Jersey

In America, things happened a little more slowly. People weren't sure the statue would ever be finished, and they often didn't understand its meaning or why it would be located in New York and not in the nation's capital, Washington, D.C.

A man named Joseph Pulitzer, who owned the *World*, a daily newspaper in New York, began to print articles about the statue. He asked people to donate whatever they could, and he promised to publish the names of every contributor in his paper. The money began to come in from working men and women, immigrants, and even school children. Five months later, the city had raised over 100,000 dollars, enough to finance the building of the base.

Joseph Pulitzer

In 1947, a postage stamp was printed to honor Joseph Pulitzer on the 100th anniversary of his birth.

Building Liberty

Bartholdi decided to make his statue out of thin sheets of copper because copper is light and easy to mold. The interior of the statue would be supported by an iron and steel framework. This would make it both light and strong so that it could be transported all the way from France to America. Because the statue was so large, Bartholdi had to work on it in sections, and he needed the help of many different artists and craftsmen.

One man who helped him, Alexandre-Gustave Eiffel, was the famous **engineer** who later built the Eiffel Tower in Paris. Eiffel designed a strong iron skeleton to support the statue's copper plates so that the statue could withstand the high winds and changes in temperature of New York Harbor.

Alexandre-Gustave Eiffel

16

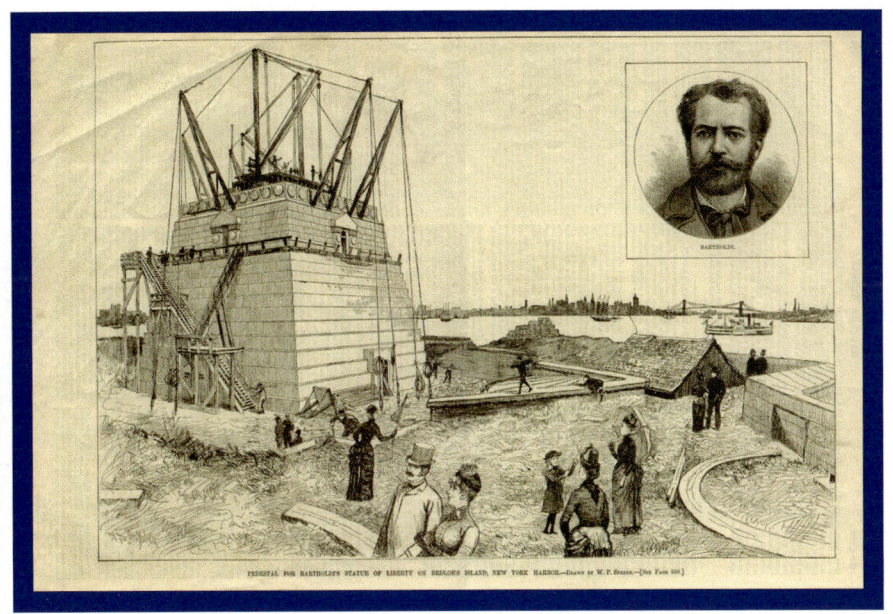

The base of the statue was constructed on top of an old military fort, Fort Wood, on Bedloe's Island.

The statue itself was completed section by section, starting with the torch and the head. For each section, workers started with a small model and then made a series of carefully measured molds of increasing size out of wood and **plaster**. Then coppersmiths used hammers to form more than 300 separate sheets of copper into the intricate shapes of Liberty's face, hands, and clothes.

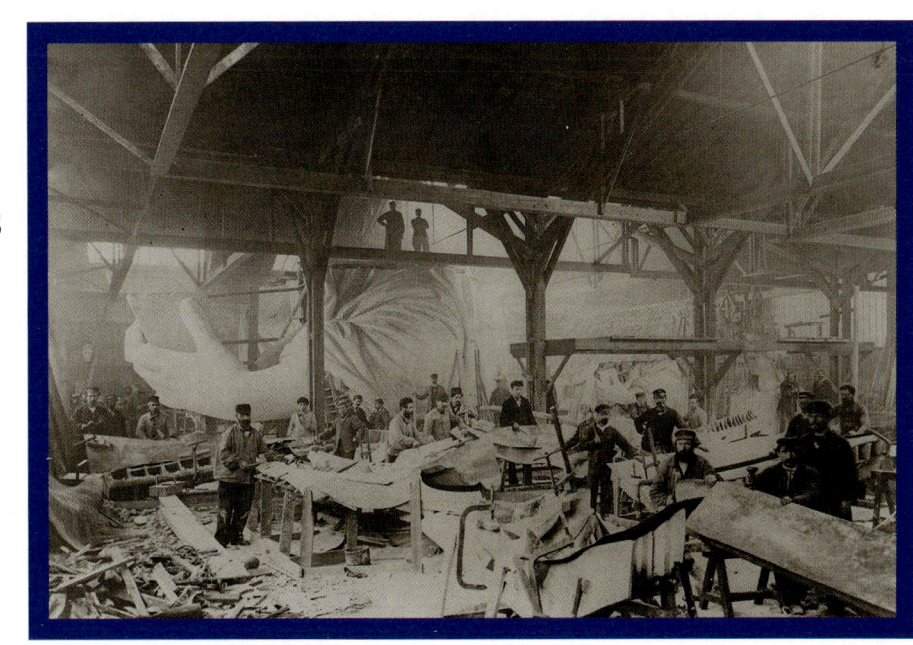

It took workers four months to put Liberty back together again in New York.

17

Gigantic Proportions

Height of statue from base to torch: 151 feet 1 inch

Total height from base of **foundation** to top of torch: 305 feet 1 inch

Length of the right arm: 42 feet

Width of one eye: 2 feet 6 inches

Length of the nose: 4 feet 6 inches

Width of the mouth: 3 feet

Length of the index finger: 8 feet

Weight of the copper: 32 tons

Weight of the steel: 125 tons

Total weight: 225 tons

Length of the tablet: 13 feet 7 inches

Length of the torch: 21 feet

Weight of fingernail: about 3.5 pounds

Weight of concrete foundation: 27,000 tons (the largest 19th century concrete structure in the United States)

Length of sandal: 25 feet

Steps from base of pedestal to crown: 354 steps

Width of the copper sheets: each 3/32-inch thick (about the thickness of two pennies put together)

The Statue's Symbols

Rays of the crown: There are seven rays in Liberty's crown to represent the seven oceans and seven continents of the world.

Tablet: Liberty's tablet is inscribed July 4, 1776, in Roman numerals. This is the date of America's independence from Britain and the date of the signing of the Declaration of Independence.

Clothing: Liberty is dressed as a classical Roman goddess to remind us of the ancient Roman Republic, the basis of America's representative form of government.

Torch: The torch symbolizes enlightenment and the light that human liberty shines around the world.

Chains: There are chains and a broken shackle at Liberty's feet. They represent breaking the bonds of slavery, which America abolished at the end of the Civil War. They also symbolize the many immigrants who have broken free from suffering and oppression in coming to America.

Liberty Arrives in America

On July 4, 1884, the statue was finished and presented to America at a ceremony in France. Then she was dismantled, packed into 214 specially made crates, and loaded aboard a French naval ship, the *Isere*. When she arrived in New York in June of 1885, the pedestal was still not ready, so the statue had to wait in storage.

21

Liberty Celebration, October 1886

Finally, on October 28, 1886, Liberty was ready. Boats full of people swarmed in the bay around the statue. President Grover Cleveland officially accepted France's gift to the American people. It was raining too hard for the fireworks to go off as planned, but three nights later when the rain stopped, they lit up the sky in a magnificent display celebrating the statue.

Did you know?

The statue's surface is made of copper, just like a penny, and originally it was the color of a shiny new penny. It looks greenish white today because over the years it has developed a **patina**, a coating that occurs naturally on the surface of copper. A patina develops when the copper metal interacts with the elements in air and rain. The patina helps protect the statue from the weather, and some think that it also adds to the statue's beauty.

Ellis Island

During the late nineteenth and early twentieth centuries, millions of **immigrants** came to America from Europe. Some came to escape poverty and hunger and to find economic opportunities in the United States. Others came to find freedom from religious and political oppression.

Beginning in 1892, Ellis Island became the official entry station for all of these people. As these immigrants entered the harbor on ships headed toward Ellis Island, they passed the Statue of Liberty. Her magnificent human form seemed to hold out the torch for them, welcoming them and offering them the light of her liberty.

Ellis Island

A Poem for Liberty

In 1883, the writings of famous American authors were put on sale to raise money for the Statue of Liberty's base. A poet named Emma Lazarus was asked to contribute a poem.

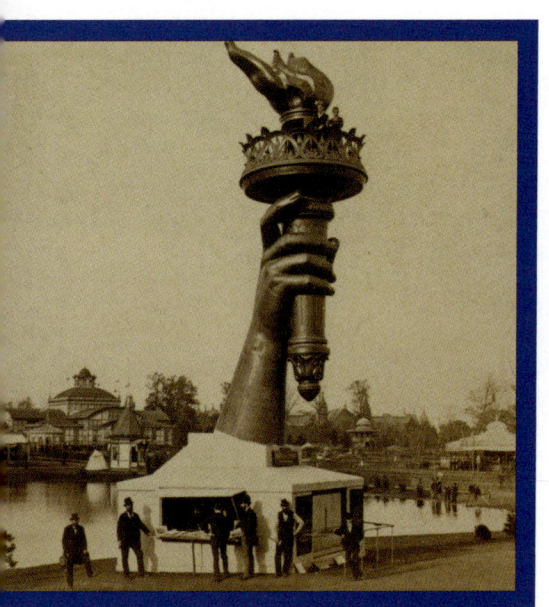

Lazarus hesitated at first, but then wrote a poem called *The New Colossus*. She was particularly concerned about Jewish immigrants fleeing from **persecution** in Russia, but her poem reaches out to all immigrants who come to America to find freedom. In the poem, she envisions the Statue of Liberty welcoming these immigrants to the golden door of America, shining her torch and lighting the way to a new life.

The New Colossus

Not like the **brazen** giant of Greek fame
With conquering limbs **astride** from land to land;
Here at our sea-washed, sunset gates shall stand
A mighty woman with a torch, whose flame
Is the imprisoned lightning, and her name
Mother of **Exiles**. From her beacon-hand
Glows world-wide welcome; her mild eyes command
The air-bridged harbor that twin cities frame,
"Keep, ancient lands, your storied **pomp**!" cries she
With silent lips. "Give me your tired, your poor,
Your huddled masses yearning to breathe free,
The wretched refuse of your teeming shore,
Send these, the homeless, **tempest-tost** to me,
I lift my lamp beside the golden door!"

Changes and Renovations

Today, the Statue of Liberty is over one hundred years old. She has stood through many storms and seasons, and her appearance has changed relatively little.

One of the things about the statue that has changed quite a bit is her torch. The torch's original lights were not very bright, and today, the old torch has been completely replaced. The new torch is made of copper and covered in gold leaf. The gold shines in the sunlight during the day and is lit by floodlights at night.

The original torch is now on display in the monument's museum.

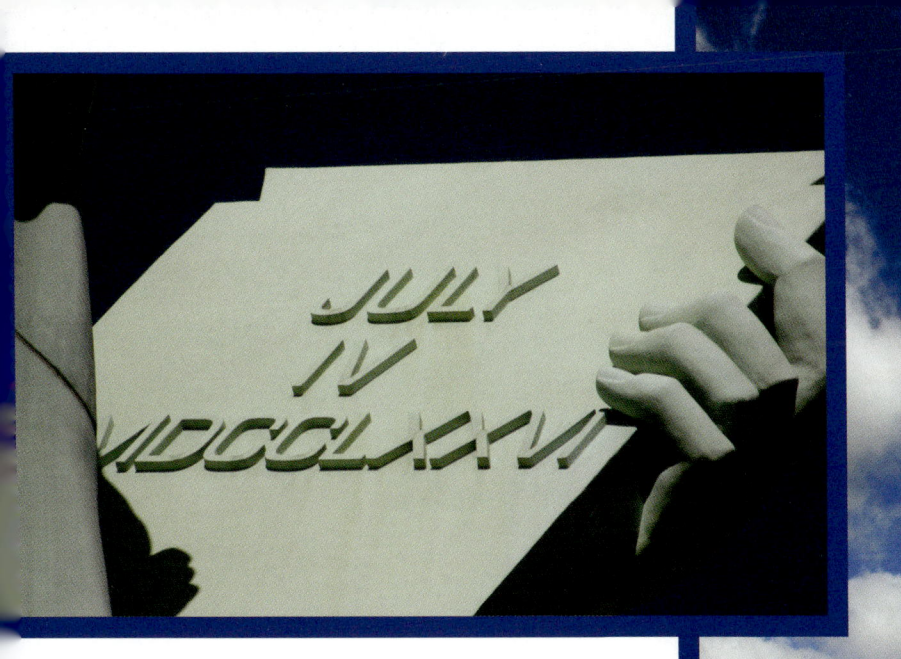

The Roman numerals on Liberty's tablet read July 4, 1776; the date the Declaration of Independence was signed.

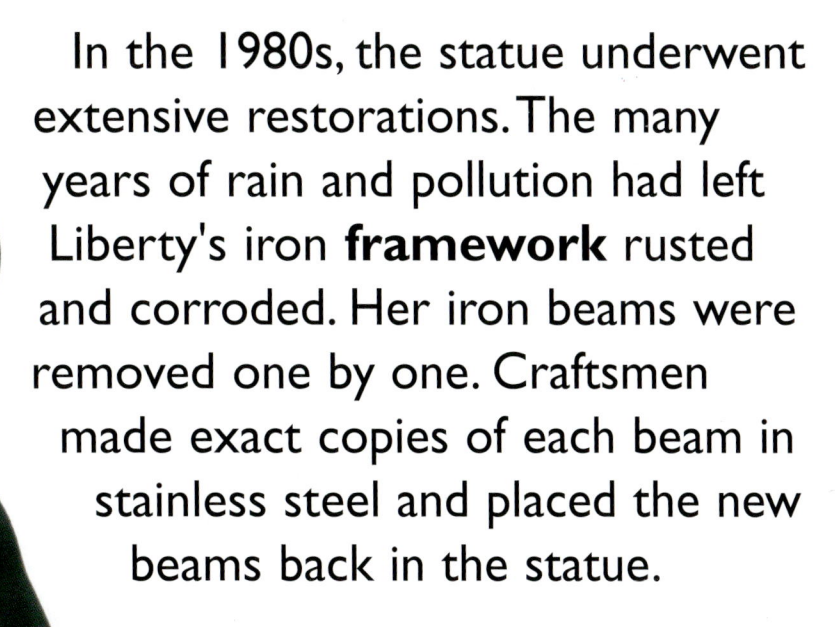

In the 1980s, the statue underwent extensive restorations. The many years of rain and pollution had left Liberty's iron **framework** rusted and corroded. Her iron beams were removed one by one. Craftsmen made exact copies of each beam in stainless steel and placed the new beams back in the statue.

29

Visiting the Statue of Liberty National Monument

In 1924, the Statue of Liberty became a National Monument. In 1956, Bedloe's Island was renamed Liberty Island, and in 1965, Ellis Island Immigration Museum became part of the Statue of Liberty National Monument.

You can reach Liberty Island only by boat. Ferry boats travel daily from Battery Place in southern Manhattan, New York. After the terrorist attacks on September 11, 2001, the island was closed for security reasons. Although the island itself re-opened to visitors in December 2001, tourists still cannot enter the statue or the pedestal.

Glossary

astride (uh-STRIYD): standing with one leg on either side of something

brazen (BRAY-zihn): made of or looking like brass

engineer (EN-jih-NEER): a person trained in a specific technology

exiles (EG-zylz): people who are separated from their country or home

framework (FRAYM-wurk): a supporting structure

foundation (faun-DAY-shun): the structure underneath a building that gives it support

immigrants (IM-i-grints): people who leave their native land in order to live in another country

patina (peh-TEE-neh): a greenish coating that appears on the surface of copper and other metals when they are exposed to air and weather

persecution (PUR-si-KYU-shun): the condition of being treated cruelly or unfairly because of race, religion, or other differences

plaster (PLAS-tur): a paste that hardens when it dries and that is used to cover a surface

pomp (PAHMP): a magnificent display

tempest-tost (TEM-pus TOST): tossed by a strong wind or storm

Further Reading

Curlee, Lynn. *Liberty*. Atheneum Books for Young Readers, 2000.

Landau, Elaine. *The Statue of Liberty*. Cornerstones of Freedom Series. Children's Press, 2004.

Hochain, Serge. *Building Liberty: A Statue Is Born*. National Geographic Children's Books, 2004.

Index

Bartholdi, Frederic Auguste   8, 9, 14
Bedloe's Island (now Liberty Island)   8, 30
Civil War   19
Cleveland, Grover   22
Declaration of Independence   6, 19
Eiffel, Alexandre-Gustave   15
Ellis Island   4, 24, 30
immigrants   4, 24, 26
Isere   20
Laboulaye, Edouard de   6
Lazarus, Emma   26
"The New Colossus"   26, 27
patina   23
Pulitzer, Joseph   13
Revolutionary War   6
Statue of Liberty National Monument
World   13

Websites

www.nps.gov/stli

www.statueofliberty.org

www.statueofliberty.net

About the Author

Holly Karapetkova, Ph. D, loves writing poems and books for kids and adults. She teaches at Marymount University and lives in the Washington, D.C., area with her husband, her son K.J., and her two dogs, Muffy and Attila.

AMERICAN SYMBOLS AND LANDMARKS

See the United States through the most well-known symbols and landmarks. The *American Symbols and Landmarks* series teaches readers about U.S. history, great leaders, and special buildings that symbolize freedom and liberty.

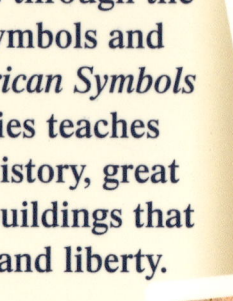

Titles In This Series:
The American Flag
The Bald Eagle
Mount Rushmore
The Statue of Liberty
The United States Capitol
The White House

ISBN 978-1-60472-975-7

Rourke Publishing